SUMMARY

D0446003

A Mind of Your Own: The Truth about Depression and How Women Can Heal Their Bodies to Reclaim Their Lives by Kelly Brogan

By High Speed Reads

© 2016 High Speed Reads

Please be advised that this is an UNOFFICIAL summary and analysis. This summary and analysis is not affiliated, authorized, approved, licensed, or endorsed by the subject book's author or publisher.

No part of this publication may be stored in a retrieval system, reproduced, or transmitted in any form or by any means, electronic, mechanical, photocopying, scanning, recording, or otherwise, except as permitted under Sections 107 or 108 of the 1976 United States Copyright Act, without either the prior written authorization from the Author or Publisher.

The author and publisher make no warranties or representations with respect to the accuracy or completeness of the contents of this book and specifically disclaim any implied warranties of merchantability or fitness for a particular purpose. The Content and price are subject to change without notice.

Table of Contents

Introduction

30 Second Summary

A Mind of Your Own will illuminate the true cause of depression in your life and give you steps to reach a point where you can be truly happy. The research Dr. Kelly Brogan presents to us is astounding and leaves no doubt that she is an expert in her field. Inside this book you will learn a new way to maintain your body thru the foods you eat. You'll learn how to prioritize restful sleep and adequate exercise. You'll learn how to turn your house and environment green, removing toxins and chemicals. Lastly you will learn to include daily meditation into your life that will clear the way for a lasting transformation.

Chapter 1: Decoding Depression

Summary

We all have an instinctive idea of what health is but many of us have lost the path to peak health. It is a national crisis that one in four American women is taking medication for mental health problems. It should be noted that only in the last few decades has depression been considered a disease and that the cure for it was chemical antidepressants, which is nowhere near the truth. Sadly we have placed our health in the hands of those that wish to profit from it.

If you only learn one lesson from this book it should be to leave your fear behind and commit to uncovering your best self, without medication. To start I want you to accept the following ideas:

1. Taking medication comes at a great cost

2. You can prevent depression

3. Your best health is not possible with medication

4. Lifestyle medicine is an effective and safe way to heal your body

5. The person with the greatest control over your health is you

Throughout this book I'll be showing you scientific proof to back those statements up and I'll also explain what lifestyle medicine is. For now, if I asked you to define depression what would you say? My guess is you'd mention "mental illness" or "mood disorders" caused by a chemical imbalance of some sort. You would be wrong. It's important to understand that depression is not a disease; it's a symptom that gives no sign of its real cause. Imagine that your finger hurts, there are many potential causes for a hurt finger but the pain is a clear sign that something is wrong, it's that simple. Similarly, depression is the pain; it's a response communicated by the body telling us that something's not right.

Have you ever wondered if there are benefits to depression? That might sound crazy but it's a good question to ask and a better question to answer. In this instance we'll focus on the topic of stress which often accompanies depression. We can describe stress as the behaviors, thoughts, physiological changes and feelings that happen as a result of the demands of life when those demands overwhelm us.

Most of us know the warning signs of stress. You may get headaches, an upset stomach, become irritable or your heart may race. You may not have thought about it this way but from an evolutionary view point stress enables us to escape from life threatening events or face them head on, fight or flight. From another point of view the stress of dealing with depression can quicken the aging process and even cause health problems. It's easy to say that stress must be managed but taking antidepressants isn't the way to do it. Don't worry if you're taking them now, the information in this book will show you how to take control of your symptoms.

Recap of Chapter 1

1. Only in the last few decades has depression been considered a disease and that the cure for it was chemical antidepressants.

2. Depression is not a disease; it's a symptom that gives no sign of its real cause.

3. Depression is a response communicated by the body telling us that something is not right.

4. Stress can be described as the behaviors, thoughts, physiological changes and feelings that happen as a result of the demands of life when those demands overwhelm us.

5. The stress of dealing with depression can quicken the aging process and even cause health problems.

Chapter 2: Truth Serum- Coming Clean About the Serotonin Myth

Summary

There is a remarkably long list of disorders and symptoms that antidepressants can be prescribed to treat. Some of which include anorexia, pain, irritable bowel, bipolar disorder, anxiety, obsessive compulsive disorder and premenstrual syndrome. There are doctors that even prescribe antidepressants for migraines and hot flashes. The belief that antidepressants correct a chemical imbalance in the brain is so widely accepted that no one even bothers to research it or question it. The fact is no human study has ever linked low serotonin levels to depression. No blood test, urine test, suicide assessment, imaging study or animal research has been able to validate a link between depression and neurotransmitter levels. Simply put, the serotonin theory of depression is a fallacy that has been propped up by manipulated data.

Antidepressants have a history of violent side effects including homicide and suicide. Other potential side effects include insomnia, abnormal bleeding, migraines, sexual dysfunction and suppressed libido. Of the top 10 most violence inducing drugs five are antidepressants. Patients that are vulnerable to these side effects are in essence playing Russian roulette with their health. It has been proven that without treatment low mood can resolve itself within 3 months and even depression can be resolved without medication in under a year for over 70% of people. Even knowing this we still run to drugs that little by little remove the body's own ability to heal itself. The challenge is that it's human nature to find the fastest path to relief, even if that path can have devastating consequences.

We must start looking at anxiety and depression as what they really are: symptoms of a body struggling to adapt to stress. As we move out of our comfort zone it will become easier for us to truly grow. This growth will include a sense of curiosity and wonder. Our most powerful tools for healing include the ability to send the body signals of safety thru meditation, diet and movement. Even exercise on its own has shown to have the same result as taking Zoloft but exercise combined with Zoloft shows diminished results. When you discover the primary causes of your symptoms, both mental and physical, and begin to address them you will be able to restore your health without drugs or psychotherapy.

Recap of Chapter 2

1. Antidepressants can be prescribed to treat anorexia, pain, irritable bowel, bipolar disorder, anxiety, obsessive compulsive disorder and premenstrual syndrome.

2. No human study has ever linked low serotonin levels to depression

3. No blood test, urine test, suicide assessment, imaging study or animal research has been able to validate a link between depression and neurotransmitter levels.

4. Potential side effects of antidepressants include insomnia, abnormal bleeding, migraines, sexual dysfunction and suppressed libido.

5. Our most powerful tools for healing include the ability to send the body signals of safety thru meditation, diet and movement.

Chapter 3: The New Biology of Depression

Summary

Inflammation is often referred to as the hidden cause of every chronic illness, from diabetes, obesity and heart disease to cancer and dementia. At the core of any healthy immune system is the capability to experience safe forms of inflammation, such as what would be triggered by a sprained ankle or paper cut. Swelling, bruising and redness are examples of inflammation we can see and feel. In this way inflammation allows the body to defend itself against potential harm. When the trigger becomes chronic, such as the body showing signs of depression, the effect on our cells can become toxic. This happens because there are no pain receptors in the brain. One important piece of information about the role of inflammation in depression is that it tends to originate in the gut.

The body absorbs nutrients from the gut with two pathways. One guides nutrients into and through the epithelial cells and the other guides nutrients between them. These cell connections are called tight junctions and are highly regulated. If they were to become compromised this would cause a condition called leaky gut. When these intestinal barriers are damaged bacteria components, cell debris and undigested food particles can sneak into the bloodstream with the effect of manifesting depressive symptoms.

A large majority of our immune system is located near our gut. It's referred to as the gut associated lymphatic tissue or GALT. The reason so much of our immune system is located near the gut is the intestinal wall which borders the outside world. This is where we have the highest chance of encountering foreign organisms and materials. If a potentially harmful substance is found in the gut every immune system cell in the body is notified and put on alert. This is why what we eat is so important to immune health and why consuming the wrong foods could spell disaster while conversely eating the right foods can be a form of health insurance.

A few of the biggest villains to gut health are listed below.

1. Gluten

2. Dairy

3. GMO's

4. Artificial Sugars

5. Antibiotics

6. NSAID's and Proton-pump inhibitors (Acid-Reflux Drugs)

True healing can be achieved by working daily to send our bodies the message that we are not in danger and we are not being attacked. That we are well supported well nourished and calm. Remember that the brain; gut and immune system are all interconnected.

Recap of Chapter 3

1. Inflammation is often referred to as the hidden cause of every chronic illness, from diabetes, obesity and heart disease to cancer and dementia.

2. Swelling, bruising and redness are all examples of inflammation we can see and feel.

3. The body absorbs nutrients from the gut with two pathways. One guides nutrients into and through the epithelial cells and the other guides nutrients between them.

4. The reason so much of our immune system is located near the gut is the intestinal wall which borders the outside world.

5. The brain, gut and immune system are all interconnected.

Chapter 4: The Great Psychiatric Pretenders

Summary

At this point you should know that depression is more than a simple brain disorder. But did you know that several undiagnosed conditions can actually look like psychiatric disorders? We'll refer to them as the psychiatric pretenders and a malfunctioning thyroid is the most common among women today. Hypothyroidism, an underperforming thyroid, affects up to 20% of all women, but only half of those women are actually diagnosed. Blood sugar imbalance is the other pretender and is very common in our society as well.

The thyroid is a butterfly shaped gland located at the base of the neck and it has many important functions such as controlling protein synthesis and the production of hormones that regulate metabolism. It also helps with growth functions, cognition, immunity and detoxification. Certain food additives and chemicals can interfere with thyroid functions, such as tap water which can contain fluoride, soda which contains emulsifiers and plastics which contain bisphenol A and its relatives. When your thyroids active hormone is functioning poorly it's likely you will experience low mood, hair loss, fatigue, constipation, low metabolism, foggy thinking, weight gain, muscle aches and dry skin. All of which are depression like symptoms. Finding problems in the thyroid is not easy as doctors don't see the immune system as a method of disease reversal and they rarely look at free hormone levels.

Your thyroids ability to function properly is at the mercy of a stress hormone that's produced by the adrenal glands, that hormone is called cortisol. When we examine which stressors mobilize the adrenals the following must be considered: birth control pills, gluten, fluoride and endocrine disruptors.

Supporting the immune system is the first step in supporting a healthy thyroid. Herbs, certain anti inflammatory vitamins, a low sugar diet and getting blood sugar under control are important tools in the war to gain full control of your health. This will be covered in greater detail later in the book. Below is a list of toxic ingredients that you should eliminate immediately from your diet.

1. unhealthy fats like processed vegetable oil

2. genetically modified foods such as soy, canola oil and corn

3. Casein, as found in milk and cheese and other dairy products

4. Sugars such as high fructose corn syrup and artificial sugars like splenda and equal

5. Gluten containing proteins as found in barley, rye and wheat

Recap of Chapter 4

1. Hypothyroidism, an underperforming thyroid, affects up to 20% of all women, but only half of those women are actually diagnosed.

2. The thyroid is a butterfly shaped gland located at the base of the neck and it has many important functions such as controlling protein synthesis and the production of hormones that regulate metabolism.

3. Finding problems in the thyroid is not easy as doctors don't see the immune system as a method of disease reversal and they rarely look at free hormone levels.

4. When your thyroids active hormone is functioning poorly it's likely you will experience low mood, hair loss, fatigue, constipation, low metabolism, foggy thinking, weight gain, muscle aches and dry skin.

5. Supporting the immune system is the first step in supporting a healthy thyroid.

Chapter 5: Why Body Lotions, Tap Water, and OTC Pain Relievers Should Come with New Warning Labels

Summary

There are certain non psychiatric drugs that can trigger symptoms of depression and im going to reveal them here along with common sources of environmental toxins that can be easily limited in our lives. We'll start with the three worst offenders, birth control, statins and acid reflux medications.

1. **Birth Control:** Oral contraceptives contribute to oxidative stress, a disastrous force in the body that is sustained by free radicals that outnumber available factors and antioxidant enzymes. They also deplete minerals, antioxidants and vitamins.

2. **Statins:** Statins are any group of drugs that attempt to reduce cholesterol and levels of fats in the blood (Lipitor, Zocor or Crestor). Many people take these drugs in hopes of avoiding a heart attack but I doubt they realize low cholesterol is linked to depression, suicide and many other neurological disorders. Statins can also cause cataracts, muscle pain, diabetes, decreased cognitive functions and sexual dysfunction.

3. **Acid Reflux Medications:** Examples include Prevacid, Protonix, Nexium and Prilosec. Stomach acid is an intrinsic factor in vitamin B12 absorption; it's critical for triggering digestive enzymes and also manages local microbial populations. Acid reflux medications can put you on a path to depression by

rendering you B12 deficient. Vitamin B12 supports the sheath around nerve fibers that lets nerve impulses conduct. When B12 is deficient it's believed to cause loss of sensation, impaired gait, signs of dementia and multiple sclerosis. When it comes to mental health and depression vitamin B12 is among the most important.

4. **Advil and other NSAIDS:** NSAID's, such as Advil, are commonly used as a treatment for fever and inflammation. These drugs reduce the amount of prostaglandins in your body. Prostaglandins support blood clotting performance, they support inflammation that is necessary for healing and they protect the stomachs lining from the destructive effects of acid. Our stomachs lining keeps our gut content out of the bloodstream. If its penetrability is raised, intestinal contents can enter the immune system which will set off inflammatory and autoimmune processes. There is a safer alternative for dealing with pain: Curcumin, otherwise known as turmeric extract, is documented to have strong anti inflammatory effects. Recent studies show that turmeric extract rivals NSAID's in managing pain associated with the menstrual cycle.

5. **Fluoride:** There have been more than 100 animal studies and 23 human studies that link fluoride to brain damage. Fluoride can calcify the pineal gland, increase the absorption of manganese and aluminum and damage the brains memory center. Not to mention baby formula mixed with tap water can include up to a 100% greater dose of fluoride than is deemed acceptable.

Recap of Chapter 5

1. Oral contraceptives contribute to oxidative stress, a disastrous force in the body that is sustained by free radicals that outnumber available factors and antioxidant enzymes.

2. Vaccines are a pharmaceutical product that are known to cause injury and death but are still recommended to the general populous.

3. Tylenol depletes the body of glutathione, the body's most vital antioxidant, which helps control inflammation in the brain and the body.

4. Low cholesterol is linked to depression, suicide and many other neurological disorders. Statins can also cause cataracts, muscle pain, diabetes, decreased cognitive functions and sexual dysfunction.

5. Vitamin B12 supports the sheath around nerve fibers that lets nerve impulses conduct. When B12 is deficient it's believed to cause loss of sensation, impaired gait, signs of dementia and multiple sclerosis.

6. NSAID's reduce the prostaglandins that protect the stomachs lining from stomach acids. Our stomachs lining keeps our gut content out of the bloodstream. If its penetrability is raised, intestinal contents can enter the immune system which will set off inflammatory and autoimmune processes.

Chapter 6: Let Food Be Thy Medicine

Summary

This chapter will focus on certain commonly consumed foods that you should eliminate from your plate and also dietary recommendations. Below I will give you the components of a depression free, health promoting diet:

1. **Eliminate Processed Food-** Processed food can be broadly described as anything in a package. Or anything with a long ingredients list. Many of the ingredients are designed to let the food have a longer shelf life and these ingredients don't overlap with our goals. A few of the problematic ingredients include Flour, which promotes unstable blood sugar and is typically made from allergenic grains or pesticide sprayed grains. Soy, corn and gluten are all considered Allergenic foods. Removing gluten from your life is easier than you think.

The Following starches and grains contain gluten: Semolina, rye, matzo, kamut, graham flour, farina, couscous, bulgur, barley, wheat germ, wheat, spelt, triticale.

The Following starches and grains are gluten free: teff, tapioca, soy, sorghum, rice, quinoa, potatoes (including sweet potatoes), millet, corn, buckwheat, amaranth, arrowroot.

The Following ingredients typically include gluten: vegetable protein, triticum vulare, triticum aestivum, secale cereal, phytosphingosine extract, natural flavoring, modified food starch, maltodextrin, hydrolyzed malt extract, hydrolysate, fermented grain extract, dextrin, amino peptide complex.

The Following foods typically include gluten: Ketchup, imitation crab meat, ice cream, hot dogs, gravy, fruit filling and puddings, fried vegetables, French fries, energy bars, egg substitute, cold cuts, breaded foods, blue cheeses, beer, bacon, baked beans, mayonnaise, marinades, oat bran (unless certified gluten free), root beer, sausage, soy sauce and teriyaki sauce, trail mix, veggie burgers, wine coolers.

Sugar- Sugar appears on almost every packaged foods ingredient list. It may be listed under a different name such as high fructose corn syrup, cane sugar or crystalline fructose but its sugar all the same. The body handles fructose differently than it handles glucose. Fructose is 7 times as likely to produce glycation end products, sticky carbohydrate aggregates that cause inflammation and oxidative stress. Besides that all types of sugar cause changes in our arteries, cell membranes, hormones, immune system and gut. If you must have some sweetness try maple syrup, honey or coconut sap sugar.

The Following ingredients typically mean sugar: dextrose, corn syrup, evaporated cane juice, invert sugar, turbinado sugar, beet sugar, maltodextrin, maltose, malt, sucrose, fructose, crystalline fructose, high fructose corn syrup.

2. **Eat Whole Foods-** Once you remove processed foods from your diet you can focus on whole, simple, pure

foods that don't often include nutrition labels: vegetables and fresh fruits, wild fish, eggs, seeds and nuts, pastured meats and traditional natural fats such as from coconut and olives.

Foods that you should buy organic: Cucumbers, hot peppers, lettuce, kale/collard greens, cherry tomatoes, potatoes, grapes, sweet bell peppers, nectarines, spinach, peaches, strawberries, celery, apples.

Foods not as important to buy organic: Cauliflower, grapefruit, sweet potatoes, papaya, cabbage, kiwi, cantaloupe, eggplant, mangoes, sweet peas (frozen), asparagus, onions, sweet corn, pineapple, avocado.

Wild Fish and Pastured Animal Products- These products come from animals that are able to eat their evolutionary predetermined natural foods and also allowed to roam free. I suggest eating organic, pastured meats: pork, beef and lamp up to 5 times a week; poultry and fish up to three times a week; but eggs each day.

Pastured Eggs- These eggs come from chickens that are allowed to roam free and eat what they would normally eat in the wild, plants and insects. Eggs are a great food and the yolks contain all the amino acids we need, not to mention minerals and vitamins.

Nuts and Seeds- All raw dry roasted nuts and seeds are good. It should be mentioned that peanuts are a legume, not a nut and they have a high risk for mold, also soy can hinder pancreatic and thyroid enzymes.

3. **Don't Avoid or Restrict Natural Fats**- I'm sure at some point you tried to avoid fats thinking it was making you fat. Many weight loss books and programs push the low cholesterol and low fat diet. It's true certain fats are bad for you, like processed fats, but not natural unmodified fats from plants or animals. Coconut oil for example is not a bad fat; it's a primary source of fat in the tropics. I recommend eliminating all commercial salad dressings as most contain vegetable oils. Instead use vinegar, olive oil or lemon.

4. **Eat Mindfully-** Most of us tend to multi task while we eat. Whether it's watching t.v., talking on the phone or working on the computer. It's important to know that multi tasking in this way will compromise your digestive processes. Try treating meal time as a way to recharge and relax. Perhaps use your less dominant hand to hold the fork to slow down your eating. Don't allow eating to be just another item on your to do list.

Recap of Chapter 6

1. Flour promotes unstable blood sugar and is typically made from allergenic grains or pesticide sprayed grains.

2. It may be listed under a different name such as high fructose corn syrup, cane sugar or crystalline fructose but its sugar

3. All types of sugar cause changes in our arteries, cell membranes, hormones, immune system and gut. If you must have some sweetness try maple syrup, honey or coconut sap sugar

4. vegetables and fresh fruits, wild fish, eggs, seeds and nuts, pastured meats and traditional natural fats such as from coconut and olives are considered whole foods.

5. Try treating meal time as a way to recharge and relax. Perhaps use your less dominant hand to hold the fork to slow down your eating. Don't allow eating to be just another item on your to do list

Chapter 7: The Power of Meditation, Sleep and Exercise

Summary

Meditation is used to cultivate a state of waking relaxation and also to increase everyday performance. I've emphasized several times now that your brain, gut, hormonal and immune systems are deeply interconnected and we must appreciate this connection if we are to have any chance at intervening or preventing depression. On a daily basis we should be sending our body the message that we are not in danger, that we are not being attacked, that we are well supported, calm and well nourished.

One reason why meditation works is that it helps stabilize blood sugar and it stimulates anti inflammatory genes. Meaning that on a physical level we become calm, cool and collected. Meditation gives us freedom from our logical selves while keeping us aware of our thoughts, feelings and senses without the negativity. In this way we are able to better deal with persistent stress and even better deal with challenges that may come our way. Below are a few techniques that are simple to learn.

1. **Practice Deep Breathing**- Deep breathing is an exercise that can be done anywhere at any time. Practicing deep breathing twice per day is a good introduction to meditation that can help when you begin more advanced techniques.

2. **Summon Feelings of Gratitude**- Focusing on specific events that bring you joy, the gratitude that you feel

towards specific people and experiences that you appreciate, while practicing deep breathing can transform your heart rate to its most optimal patterns (those associated with peak mental performance and calm relaxation).

3. **Try Kundalini Yoga**- Kundalini yoga is regarded as the most thorough of yoga traditions, it combines mantra, physical exercises, meditation and breathing techniques. It gives you the ability to get out of your own way and harness your own power and bring the experience of joy into your life. If feeling alive again and optimizing your consciousness interests you give kundalini a try, visit www.spiritvoyage.com to see videos of various techniques in practice or visit www.kundaliniresearchinstitute.org for the kundalini research institute.

There are 2 more powerful habits to maintain to achieve overall wellness, sweat inducing exercise and regular restful sleep. We'll start with restful sleep as sleep deprivation can garner serious consequences, including depression. Sleeping six or less hours per night reduces alertness by about a third, and can negatively affect your ability to perform basic bodily functions similar to alcohol's affect on the body. How can you free yourself from insomnia and maximize your sleep? I've given a few ideas below.

- **Know your number**- We all have different needs, find out how much sleep is right for you by choosing an optimal wake up time then going to sleep 9 hours before it. After a week you should be waking up before your alarm.

- **Unplug to Recharge**- Use the thirty minutes before you climb into bed to prepare for sleep and unwind. An Epsom salt bath while listening to soothing music should have a noticeable calming effect.

- **Tea Time**- Try chamomile or valerian tea's, both of which are known for their calming effects.

- **Prioritize a premidnight bedtime**- The most rejuvenating hours of sleep happen before midnight, you should be in bed ideally by 10pm.

- **Minimize blue light from electronics**- This wavelength of light hinders melatonin production and stimulates the alert systems of the brain.

- **Flip the switch**- Try sleeping with your cell phone on airplane mode and make sure it's at least 6 feet from your bed.

- **Go dark**- Keep your room cool, clean and try using a sleep mask or blackout shades.

- **Do not disturb**- The bedroom should be reserved for sex and sleep. If you're not able to fall asleep within 20 minutes get up and do some breathing exercises or read, after 20 minutes try going back to sleep. Repeat this as needed.

- **Try botanicals noted to help with sleep**- The following herbs are helpful. Passionflower, valerian, magnolia and ashwagandha. These can be taken as tinctures or dried in capsules.

It's very important to take control of your sleeping habits as sleep problems are typically the first sign of ill health. Next we'll take a look at exercise, nature's antidepressant. Exercising can bring you more energy, improve your self worth, reverse aging, stave off depression and it even supports emotional stability. Exercise also improves body tone and strength, digestion, metabolism and bone density. If you're not already on one I ask that you start an exercise program. The benefits are many and it can be enjoyable when you find the right exercises for you

Recap of Chapter 7

1. Meditation is used to cultivate a state of waking relaxation and also to increase everyday performance.

2. On a daily basis we should be sending our body the message that we are not in danger, that we are not being attacked, that we are well supported, calm and well nourished.

3. One reason why meditation works is that it helps stabilize blood sugar and it stimulates anti inflammatory genes. Meaning that on a physical level we become calm, cool and collected.

4. Sleeping six or less hours per night reduces alertness by about a third, and can negatively affect your ability to perform basic bodily functions similar to alcohol's affect on the body.

5. Exercising can bring you more energy, improve your self worth, reverse aging, stave off depression and it even supports emotional stability.

Chapter 8: Clean House

Summary

No matter where you live or how old you are, every US citizen contains noticeable levels of synthetic chemicals. Dust particles grab onto chemicals in the air and travel north to colder climates. This is why humans thousands of miles away from sources of pollution show symptoms of contamination. Similarly waters that are thousands of miles away from pollutants can have chemicals carried to them by water currents and jet streams. There's no way for us to know how many of these chemicals exist or even how harmful they are, especially after they combine. It's also impossible to rely on politicians and laws to keep you safe when there are a myriad of political interests.

There are steps we can take to protect ourselves. It may seen an impossible task to clear questionable products from your home and replace them with safer products but the goal is to do the best you can. A simple first step is to buy products as close to their natural state as you can, these include items that haven't been manufactured, treated, infused with chemicals or processed in any way. A few helpful sites are www.ewg.org , www.fearlessparent.org , www.ireadlabelsforyou.com and www.thehealthyhomeeconomist.com .

Waiting until a product is labeled harmful when we can limit or remove them from our lives now would be a mistake. Below is a guide to help you.

In the kitchen:

- Avoid canned foods as they are often lined with BPA laden coating.

- Avoid non stick cookware and pans as they contain perfluorooctanoic acid which is labeled a likely carcinogen. Safe alternatives are ceramic, glass or cast iron cookware.

- Don't put hot foods in plastic and ditch the microwave. Foods can absorb chemicals that are released by plastic.

- Stop using plastic water bottles; instead buy reusable bottles made of stainless steel or glass.

In the Bathroom:

- Be wary of vinyl shower curtains.

- Visit www.ewg.org for lists of alternatives to your favorite items.

- Sephora has a line of chemical free cosmetics that are worth looking into

- Only purchase sunscreens that are free of oxybenzone and contain non micronized zinc such as the badger brand.

- Bite Blocker and California baby bug sprays both use natural alternatives to harmful chemicals.

- Deodorants, douches, washes and wipes contain dyes, parabens and chemicals under the "fragrance" label.

- Pads and tampons contain pesticides, furans and dioxins that are known to cause cancer and reproductive problems.

- A better option is to use organic feminine items or inert methods such as Gladrags.
- Instead of hand sanitizers use an all natural essential oil based product.

General Household Goods:

- Wipe down windowsills and wet mop floors weekly.
- When you buy disinfectants, detergents, stain removers or any household cleaner make sure to choose the ones that are free of synthetic chemicals. The fewer items on the ingredients list the better.
- The easiest all purpose cleaner to use is 2 cups of water with 1 teaspoon of vinegar.
- Be leery of toys made before 2009 as they potentially contain treated materials and dangerous plastics.
- Try to keep plants in your home as they will naturally detoxify your environment. A few good examples are aloe vera, spider plants, Boston ferns, English ivies, philodendrons and chrysanthemums.
- Install HEPA air filters and keep your home well ventilated.
- I recommend buying a household water filter for your drinking and cooking purposes and even for bathing. Reverse osmosis and carbon filters are my favorites.
- You can reduce your exposure to the radiation your phone or tablet puts out by using a headset instead of putting it up to your ear and keeping your phone or tablet several feet from your body during sleep and when not in use.

To the pregnant women, women with children and those that plan to have children the notes mentioned in this chapter are paramount to your child's health as well as your own so please take them seriously. The steps mentioned will help maintain your mental wellness and overall health and that of your child.

Recap of Chapter 8

1. No matter where you live or how old you are, every US citizen contains noticeable levels of synthetic chemicals.

2. A simple first step is to buy products as close to their natural state as you can, these include items that haven't been manufactured, treated, infused with chemicals or processed in any way.

3. A few helpful sites are www.ewg.org, www.fearlessparent.org, www.ireadlabelsforyou.com and www.thehealthyhomeeconomist.com.

4. Children are likely to be more vulnerable to the radiation from your phones and tablets.

5. Try to keep plants in your home as they will naturally detoxify your environment. A few good examples are aloe vera, spider plants, Boston ferns, English ivies, philodendrons and chrysanthemums.

6. The easiest all purpose cleaner to use is 2 cups of water with 1 teaspoon of vinegar.

Chapter 9: Testing and Supplementing

Summary

Vitamin B12 is a basic building block of life, it protects the nervous system and the brain, it makes nerve cell lining and red blood cells. It also keeps your immune system running properly and regulates mood and rest cycles. A deficiency of vitamin B12 can cause depression, memory loss, paranoia, delusions, loss of smell, loss of taste and even incontinence. Mothers that are deficient in vitamin B12 have a higher chance of passing neurological symptoms, such as developmental delays, lethargy and delayed motor development, on to their baby. It's normal in my practice to determine my patients B12 levels by ordering a simple blood test. B12 can easily be replaced in the body by a non prescription tablet or with a prescribed injection.

Testing and supplementing are two key features of my general protocol. This means ordering specific lab tests to help rule out underlying medical conditions and to see what noninvasive therapies and supplements might help you. Below I will give you a list of tests I typically use with my patients.

1. **Vitamin D levels** via 250H AND 1,25: ideally 250H should be between 50 and 80 ng/mL while 1,25 should be simply be within normal range.

2. **Fasting glucose/insulin/HbA1C** (hemoglobin A1C): These tests are used to check your blood sugar. Your HbA1C values should ideally be between 4.8 and 5.2 percent. Fasting glucose should be between 70 and 80 mg/dl and insulin should be below 6 IU/ml.

3. **Hs-CRP** (High Sensitive C reactive protein) in blood: Results between 0.00 and 1.0mg/L are optimal.

4. **Vitamin B12 levels in the blood:** This measures serum B12 levels. Its best to be above 600 pg/mL (pictogram/milliliter)

5. **Homocysteine levels in blood:** This is a more accurate test for vitamin B12 deficiency; optimal levels are between 7 and 10 micromoles per liter of blood.

6. **The MTHFR genetic test:** One mutation signifies your enzyme is operating at 70%; two means your possibly down to 30%.

7. **Thyroid function tests: TSH, free T4, free T3, reverse T3, thyroid peroxidase antibodies and thyroglobulin antibodies** – This group of tests shows how well your thyroid is functioning and whether or not your immune system is wrongly attacking the gland.

You can also consider the following:

1. **Salivary cortisol:** This test measures the stress hormone cortisol at 4 times during the day. You'll simply be told to spit into a tube 4 times throughout the day then mail it to the lab.

2. **Stool culture, PCR, and proteomic testing:** The purpose of this test is to detect absorption issues, imbalances in your gut microbiota, parasites and gut inflammation.

3. **Urinary organic acid test:** This test will give you a view into the cellular metabolic processes of your

body. The purpose being to locate any defects in your body's metabolism.

You can simply go elsewhere if your doctor won't order these tests. You have to be your own advocate and insist on this baseline analysis. Now let's move on to supplements, it would be great if we lived in a world where supplements weren't necessary but sadly that's not the case. Taking certain supplements will almost always improve your health and work to keep you healthy. The basic supplements you should consider are:

- **Activated B complex:** these vitamins are needed for healthy hair, eyes, skin, liver and they assist the nervous system.

- **Selenium:** Ideal for depressive and anxious people that have low thyroid function.

- **Iodine:** From a supplement that contains Atlantic kelp

- **Zinc:** This mineral helps control the body and brains response to stress.

- **Magnesium:** I recommend magnesium glycinate over the other types.

- **Fatty Acids:** In the form of cod liver and fish oil supplements.

- **Evening Primrose Oil:** Beneficial for brittle hair, premenstrual syndrome, eczema, multiple sclerosis and menopausal symptoms.

- **Cod Liver Oil:** I recommend finding a supplement that contains a five to one ratio of vitamin A to vitamin D.

- **Betaine HCL:** Helps boost your stomachs ability to digest.

- **Digestive Enzymes:** There are many options but focus on the ones that are plant sourced and contain a mix of enzymes like lipases, proteases and amylase.

- **Adrenal and Hypothalamus Glandulars:** Hypothalamus helps repair communication between the glands and the brain. Adrenals help fight depression symptoms.

Lifestyle changes can seem difficult at first glance. You've just processed a lot of information so take a deep breath and let it settle into your mind. If you haven't already started to make some of the changes we've talked about in previous chapters I recommend you begin now. In the next chapter I will give you my four week program that was created to restore your brain and body back to peak condition and also shift your diet. This program does have physical benefits but you will also notice other rewards. A few include ending depression, higher self esteem, more confidence, feeling younger, better able to handle stress, more motivation and an overall youthful feel. Get ready to watch positive changes flow into your life.

Recap of Chapter 9

1. Vitamin B12 is a basic building block of life, it protects the nervous system and the brain, it makes nerve cell lining and red blood cells.

2. A deficiency of vitamin B12 can cause depression, memory loss, paranoia, delusions, loss of smell, loss of taste and even incontinence.

3. B12 can easily be replaced in the body by a non prescription tablet or with a prescribed injection.

4. Lab tests can help rule out underlying medical conditions and also give you an idea of what noninvasive therapies and supplements might help you.

5. Taking certain supplements will almost always improve your health and work to keep you healthy.

6. The 4 week program does have physical benefits but you will also notice other rewards. A few include ending depression, higher self esteem, more confidence, feeling younger, better able to handle stress, more motivation and an overall youthful feel.

Chapter 10: 4 Weeks to a Natural High

Summary

For the next four weeks I'll take you step by step in an effort to bring everything you've learned together. I know that quitting pizza, bread, pasta and pastries is going to be tough for some people; change in general is tough so that's to be expected but I want to assure you it is possible, you just have to make the commitment. Within a week I believe you will sleep better, feel less anxious and have improved energy. As always you should check with your doctor before beginning any new program, especially if you have serious health issues. Over the next 30 days you will reach 4 important goals:

1. You will learn a new way to maintain your body through the foods you eat.

2. You will learn how to turn your house and environment green, removing toxins and chemicals.

3. You will learn to include daily meditation into your life that will clear the way for a lasting transformation.

4. You will learn to prioritize restful sleep and adequate exercise.

The program has been split up into 4 weeks, as listed above, each week focusing on one specific goal. Week 1 will focus on a dietary detox and this will continue for the full 30 days. Week 2 is the home detox where you'll learn to turn your house green. Week 3's focus will be peace of mind and this will hopefully be a lifelong habit. Week 4's focus will be sleep and movement and all you will need to do is follow my simple guidelines. This program was made to be as easy to follow as possible so let's jump in.

Week 1: Dietary Detox

This diet won't require you to limit fat intake, count calories or worry about portion sizes. You will simply eat until your content. This month you will also eliminate grains (except buckwheat and quinoa), dairy, white potatoes, white rice, beans and corn. They can be re introduced on month 2 and beyond. During week 1 try to focus on understanding your new eating habits and for the first 2 weeks try and avoid eating out if possible. Next make sure to drink half your body weight in ounces of water each daily. If you weigh 130 pounds you should drink 65 ounces daily, 8 glasses of water at 8 ounces each, of purified water, no tap. You shouldn't drink fruit drinks, soda, tea, coffee or alcohol of any kind. After the initial 30 days tea, coffee and alcohol can be reintroduced.

We all want a snack from time to time so the following are acceptable:

- Grass fed jerky
- Bone broth
- Berries with coconut milk
- Seaweed (Atlantic is preferred)
- Lactofermented vegetables
- 2 soft boiled eggs
- Chopped raw veggies
- Raw nuts or seeds minus peanuts
- Roasted beef, chicken or turkey dipped in mustard

- Half of an ovocado with salt, pepper, lemon and oil

Example Menu for the Week

Remember removing dairy, grains, soy, corn and processed sugar is the most important part of the first 30 days. You should also avoid white rice and white potatoes the first month as well and don't forget to drink your filtered water daily. This is what a typical week will look like.

Monday

Breakfast: 2 strips pastured bacon, 2 pastured eggs soft poached with spinach, 1 cup boiled root veggies such as beets, carrots or sweet potatoes with ghee and a squeeze of lemon.

Lunch: Organic roasted wild fish or chicken with a side of vegetables sautéed in garlic and leafy greens.

Dinner: Sweet potatoes covered in meat sauce, steamed asparagus and broccoli with salt, olive oil and lemon.

Dessert: 1 whole fruit with a little honey.

Tuesday

Breakfast: KB Smoothie

Lunch: Fresh garden salad with medium rare grass fed beef

Dinner: Quinoa covered in chicken curry and all you can eat roasted vegetables

Dessert: A couple squares of dark chocolate

Wednesday

Breakfast: Seed cereal with voluntary Hardboiled egg with sea salt and a squeeze of lemon

Lunch: Skinless and boneless sardines with a side of kimchi or sauerkraut with an avocado topped with apple cider vinegar, salt and olive oil

Dinner: Cauliflower rice with Ghee poached salmon and zucchini sautéed in coconut oil

Dessert: Avocado chocolate mousse with honey and cinnamon on top

Thursday

Breakfast: Ghee with paleo pancakes

Lunch: Grilled chicken or fish on top of a garden salad

Dinner: Roasted root veggies with grilled steak

Dessert: Coconut crack bars

Friday

Breakfast: Cumin and ground beef with zucchini

Lunch: Kelly's chef's salad

Dinner: Quinoa with sautéed collard greens and Rosemary mustard lamb chops

Dessert: Coconut milk with golden tea

Saturday

Breakfast: KB Smoothie

Lunch: Prosciutto rolls (arugula tossed in olive oil and lemon juice then wrapped in prosciutto)

Dinner: Coconut cauliflower rice with Nonna's fried chicken

Dessert: Honey nut bars

Sunday

Breakfast: 2 strips pastured bacon, 2 pastured eggs soft poached with spinach and 1 cup boiled root veggies such as beets, carrots or sweet potatoes.

Lunch: Butternut squash lasagna minus the lasagna

Dinner: Sautéed capers and red cabbage with meatloaf

Dessert: A couple squares of dark chocolate drizzled with almond butter (1 tablespoon)

When we begin to remove the processed foods from our lives we can start the journey to find the diet that best suits us. By simply listening to your body, finding the diet that balances your physiology and compliments your nervous system will be unavoidable.

Week 2: Home Detox

During this week I encourage you to go back to chapter 8 and begin cleaning up your house and start to make it as green as possible. You can begin easily by exchanging toxic toiletries, beauty products, cleaning supplies and cosmetics for natural alternatives. Also make sure to bring in plants such as those listed in chapter 8 to detoxify the air in your home. Lastly place water filters on your showerheads and sinks this week.

Week 3: Peace of Mind

At this point in the 30 day plan you should be feeling a bit better. Are your thoughts clearer? Are you lighter on your feet? Perhaps those depression symptoms have lessened. This week we have 2 goals, the first is to start taking your supplements and the second is to begin practicing daily meditation. For meditation please refer back to chapter 7 and find the method that fits you best. The supplements listed in chapter 9 can be purchased at most any drugstore, supermarket, health food store or even online. I have included a list of my favorite brands at www.Kellybroganmd.com to help.

Week 4: Movement and Sleep

If you don't already have an exercise routine it's time to get one started. If you're a beginner you can start with a minimum of 5 minutes of burst exercise and work up to 15 at least three times per week. This can be done by walking and varying your speed, slow to fast, or increase intensity by walking up stairs or a hill. You can also use online exercise videos in your home or office.

If you already have an exercise routine try to increase your workouts to at least 30 minutes per day 5 days per week. You can also switch things up and try yoga or a dance class. Whatever keeps you motivated is acceptable. Make a point to schedule your workout days in a calendar to hold yourself accountable. If you're short on time try splitting up your routine into smaller chunks, take the stairs instead of the elevator, limit the time you remain seated by walking around even when on the phone and perhaps park further away from your building. Moving benefits your body as well as your mood.

You should also be focusing on your sleep this week. Try to get at least 7 hours of sleep each night, that's the minimum if you want your hormones to fluctuate normally in your body. For more information on mastering your sleep please review chapter 7.

In Closing

If you ever feel like you're regressing simply redo this 4 week program. Even only doing two weeks of the program can relieve symptoms brought on by cheats at a wedding, vacation or dinner party. The goal of this book is to guide you in making better decisions that will let you participate in life to its fullest extent. I truly hope that I've given you lots of ideas that will at least begin to make a difference.

Recap of Chapter 10

1. As always you should check with your doctor before beginning any new program, especially if you have serious health issues

2. Week 1 will focus on a dietary detox and this will continue for the full 30 days. Week 2 is the home detox where you'll learn to turn your house green. Week 3's focus will be peace of mind and this will hopefully be a lifelong habit. Week 4's focus will be sleep and movement and all you will need to do is follow my simple guidelines.

3. Make sure to drink half your body weight in ounces of water each daily. If you weigh 130 pounds you should drink 65 ounces daily, 8 glasses of water at 8 ounces each, of purified water, no tap

4. Removing dairy, grains, soy, corn and processed sugar is the most important part of the first 30 days. You should also avoid white rice and white potatoes the first month as well and don't forget to drink your filtered water daily

5. Make sure to bring in plants such as those listed in chapter 8 to detoxify the air in your home. Place water filters on your showerheads and sinks

6. A list of my favorite supplement brands can be found at www.Kellybroganmd.com

7. Make a point to schedule your workout days in a calendar to hold yourself accountable

8. Try to get at least 7 hours of sleep each night, that's the minimum if you want your hormones to fluctuate normally in your body

Important Facts Recap

Recap of Chapter 1: Decoding Depression

1. Only in the last few decades has depression been considered a disease and that the cure for it was chemical antidepressants.

2. Depression is not a disease; it's a symptom that gives no sign of its real cause.

3. Depression is a response communicated by the body telling us that something is not right.

4. Stress can be described as the behaviors, thoughts, physiological changes and feelings that happen as a result of the demands of life when those demands overwhelm us.

5. The stress of dealing with depression can quicken the aging process and even cause health problems.

Recap of Chapter 2: Truth Serum: Coming Clean About the Serotonin Myth

1. Antidepressants can be prescribed to treat anorexia, pain, irritable bowel, bipolar disorder, anxiety, obsessive compulsive disorder and premenstrual syndrome.

2. No human study has ever linked low serotonin levels to depression

3. No blood test, urine test, suicide assessment, imaging study or animal research has been able to validate a link between depression and neurotransmitter levels.

4. Potential side effects of antidepressants include insomnia, abnormal bleeding, migraines, sexual dysfunction and suppressed libido.

5. Our most powerful tools for healing include the ability to send the body signals of safety thru meditation, diet and movement.

Recap of Chapter 3: The New Biology of Depression

1. Inflammation is often referred to as the hidden cause of every chronic illness, from diabetes, obesity and heart disease to cancer and dementia.

2. Swelling, bruising and redness are all examples of inflammation we can see and feel.

3. The body absorbs nutrients from the gut with two pathways. One guides nutrients into and through the epithelial cells and the other guides nutrients between them.

4. The reason so much of our immune system is located near the gut is the intestinal wall which borders the outside world.

5. The brain, gut and immune system are all interconnected.

Recap of Chapter 4: The Great Psychiatric Pretenders

1. Hypothyroidism, an underperforming thyroid, affects up to 20% of all women, but only half of those women are actually diagnosed.

2. The thyroid is a butterfly shaped gland located at the base of the neck and it has many important functions such as controlling protein synthesis and the production of hormones that regulate metabolism.

3. Finding problems in the thyroid is not easy as doctors don't see the immune system as a method of disease reversal and they rarely look at free hormone levels.

4. When your thyroids active hormone is functioning poorly it's likely you will experience low mood, hair loss, fatigue, constipation, low metabolism, foggy thinking, weight gain, muscle aches and dry skin.

5. Supporting the immune system is the first step in supporting a healthy thyroid.

Recap of Chapter 5: Why Body Lotions, Tap Water, and OTC Pain Relievers Should Come with New Warning Labels

1. Oral contraceptives contribute to oxidative stress, a disastrous force in the body that is sustained by free radicals that outnumber available factors and antioxidant enzymes.

2. Vaccines are a pharmaceutical product that are known to cause injury and death but are still recommended to the general populous.

3. Tylenol depletes the body of glutathione, the body's most vital antioxidant, which helps control inflammation in the brain and the body.

4. Low cholesterol is linked to depression, suicide and many other neurological disorders. Statins can also cause cataracts, muscle pain, diabetes, decreased cognitive functions and sexual dysfunction.

5. Vitamin B12 supports the sheath around nerve fibers that lets nerve impulses conduct. When B12 is deficient it's believed to cause loss of sensation, impaired gait, signs of dementia and multiple sclerosis.

6. NSAID's reduce the prostaglandins that protect the stomachs lining from stomach acids. Our stomachs lining keeps our gut content out of the bloodstream. If its penetrability is raised, intestinal contents can enter the immune system which will set off inflammatory and autoimmune processes.

Recap of Chapter 6: Let Food Be Thy Medicine

1. Flour promotes unstable blood sugar and is typically made from allergenic grains or pesticide sprayed grains.

2. It may be listed under a different name such as high fructose corn syrup, cane sugar or crystalline fructose but its sugar

3. All types of sugar cause changes in our arteries, cell membranes, hormones, immune system and gut. If you must have some sweetness try maple syrup, honey or coconut sap sugar

4. vegetables and fresh fruits, wild fish, eggs, seeds and nuts, pastured meats and traditional natural fats such as from coconut and olives are considered whole foods.

5. Try treating meal time as a way to recharge and relax. Perhaps use your less dominant hand to hold the fork to slow down your eating. Don't allow eating to be just another item on your to do list

Recap of Chapter 7: The Power of Meditation, Sleep, and Exercise

1. Meditation is used to cultivate a state of waking relaxation and also to increase everyday performance.

2. On a daily basis we should be sending our body the message that we are not in danger, that we are not being attacked, that we are well supported, calm and well nourished.

3. One reason why meditation works is that it helps stabilize blood sugar and it stimulates anti inflammatory genes. Meaning that on a physical level we become calm, cool and collected.

4. Sleeping six or less hours per night reduces alertness by about a third, and can negatively affect your ability to perform basic bodily functions similar to alcohol's affect on the body.

5. Exercising can bring you more energy, improve your self worth, reverse aging, stave off depression and it even supports emotional stability.

Recap of Chapter 8: Clean House

1. No matter where you live or how old you are, every US citizen contains noticeable levels of synthetic chemicals.

2. A simple first step is to buy products as close to their natural state as you can, these include items that haven't been manufactured, treated, infused with chemicals or processed in any way.

3. A few helpful sites are www.ewg.org , www.fearlessparent.org , www.ireadlabelsforyou.com and www.thehealthyhomeeconomist.com .

4. Children are likely to be more vulnerable to the radiation from your phones and tablets.

5. Try to keep plants in your home as they will naturally detoxify your environment. A few good examples are aloe vera, spider plants, boston ferns, English ivies, philodendrons and chrysanthemums.

6. The easiest all purpose cleaner to use is 2 cups of water with 1 teaspoon of vinegar.

Recap of Chapter 9: Testing and Supplementing

1. Vitamin B12 is a basic building block of life, it protects the nervous system and the brain, it makes nerve cell lining and red blood cells.

2. A deficiency of vitamin B12 can cause depression, memory loss, paranoia, delusions, loss of smell, loss of taste and even incontinence.

3. B12 can easily be replaced in the body by a non prescription tablet or with a prescribed injection.

4. Lab tests can help rule out underlying medical conditions and also give you an idea of what noninvasive therapies and supplements might help you.

5. Taking certain supplements will almost always improve your health and work to keep you healthy.

6. The 4 week program does have physical benefits but you will also notice other rewards. A few include ending depression, higher self esteem, more confidence, feeling younger, better able to handle stress, more motivation and an overall youthful feel.

Recap of Chapter 10: 4 Weeks to a Natural High

1. As always you should check with your doctor before beginning any new program, especially if you have serious health issues

2. Week 1 will focus on a dietary detox and this will continue for the full 30 days. Week 2 is the home detox

where you'll learn to turn your house green. Week 3's focus will be peace of mind and this will hopefully be a lifelong habit. Week 4's focus will be sleep and movement and all you will need to do is follow my simple guidelines.

3. Make sure to drink half your body weight in ounces of water each daily. If you weigh 130 pounds you should drink 65 ounces daily, 8 glasses of water at 8 ounces each, of purified water, no tap

4. Removing dairy, grains, soy, corn and processed sugar is the most important part of the first 30 days. You should also avoid white rice and white potatoes the first month as well and don't forget to drink your filtered water daily

5. Make sure to bring in plants such as those listed in chapter 8 to detoxify the air in your home. Place water filters on your showerheads and sinks

6. A list of my favorite supplement brands can be found at www.Kellybroganmd.com

7. Make a point to schedule your workout days in a calendar to hold yourself accountable

8. Try to get at least 7 hours of sleep each night, that's the minimum if you want your hormones to fluctuate normally in your body

Discussion Questions to Get You Thinking

1. What are a few signs of depression that you have experienced in your own life?

2. Name 3 potential side effects of antidepressants?

3. What is our most powerful tool for healing?

4. Name 2 examples of inflammation we can see and feel?

5. Why is so much of our immune system located near the gut?

6. Name 2 disorders linked to low cholesterol?

7. Name 4 examples of whole foods?

8. Name 2 benefits of exercising?

9. What item has the ability to naturally detoxify your home?

10. What is the minimum number of hours you should be sleeping each night?

11. How much water should you be drinking daily?

About High Speed Reads

Here at High Speed Reads our goal is to save you time by providing the best summaries possible. We stand out from our competitors by not only including all of the pertinent facts from the subject book but also discussion questions to get you thinking, easy to follow summaries of each chapter including a list of chapter highlights and even a 30 second summary of the entire book.

As you can see we go above and beyond to make your purchase a pleasant one. If you learned something beneficial from this book please leave a positive review so others can benefit as well. Lastly if you haven't yet make sure you purchase the subject book.